AN
EXALTATION
OF
GODDESSES

⁊

POEMS FOR THE DIVINE FEMININE

AN
EXALTATION
OF
GODDESSES

❧

POEMS FOR THE DIVINE FEMININE

Coordinated by Annie Finch

www.poetrywitch.com

ISBN# 978-1-7373075-0-1

Coordinated by Annie Finch

Cover Art: "Green Goddess Mandala"
by Alicja Barcikowska

Cover Design by Diane Lee Moomey and Annie Finch

Dedicated to the beloved memory of

Patricia Monaghan

Poet, Scholar, Priestess, & Co-Founder,
Association for the Study of Women and Mythology

TABLE OF CONTENTS

AN EXALTATION OF GODDESSES

EDITOR'S NOTE

The seed for this book was sown when Sid Reger of the Association for the Study of Women and Mythology asked if I'd coordinate a poetry session for ASWM's upcoming online Symposium. Sid had barely finished her query when "An Exaltation of Goddesses" sprang to life in my mind and my heart: 13 voices from many perspectives, joining in a poetic ritual theater celebration of the the Sacred Feminine.

Much, if not most, of the theater ever performed on our planet has been spoken in the rhythmical language we call poetry—an embodiment of language through ear, mouth, and heart. After having long performed my own poetry under the rubric of Poetry Witch Ritual Theater, it was a beautiful experience to invite others into PWRT thanks to the magic of the Web. I asked 12 other poets to perform a poem to a Goddess and write a meditation on Her, and the show and this book are the result.

I encourage you to read these poems aloud, with or without watching the show (which is available for viewing on the ASWM website). Thank you for adding *your* energy to the intersection of poetry, magic, and performance—a place it seems the Goddess feels very much at home.

Love and blessings,

Annie Finch

Judy Grahn

TO THE MOTHER OF ALL BOWLS

some bowls are cool
to the touch
some bowls are full of stew
some bowls don't hold
too much
what kind of bowl are you

though made of porcelain
some bowls last tens of centuries
though made of solid gold some bowls
change in a flash meltdown

some bowls age in penitentiaries
some begging bowls sit out on the ground
some bowls sing.......
some bowls get passed around
for everyone to drink

some bowls get smashed
in the kitchen sink
some bowls stand still in the old bowl museum
some bowls go to every pot luck

some bowls overflow
some bowls suck it up
some bowls clutch ash in the mausoleum
some bowls hold hospital suffering

circling bowls alleviate
envy
water bowls consecrate
nativity
burning bowls emulate

eternity
flower bowls re-create
proclivity
red garuthi bowls
soak up soak up soak up
negativity

some bowls spill out in offering
some bowls transform
some bowls bring about a sea storm
some bowls say bowls
witness everything

She loves all bowls
She makes

all bowls break
all bowls return to her

the Mother of all bowls

dishes up love,
that's why the love
is unconditional
unconditional love
belongs to bowls

ABOUT ARURU

The goddess my poem describes is Aruru, an aspect of Ninmah (later Ninhursaga), great earth mother of ancient Sumer and one of the seven elemental gods. For a while after the elements came into being, the created world hummed along with wind and light, sky and earth, river and ocean all in interactive motion. As time passed, the gods grew weary with their busy tasks running the cosmos and despaired of finding what could spare them and allow some rest. Aruru stepped in and created fourteen human beings out of blood and clay, with the designated functions of assisting the gods. The blood was supplied by one of the minor gods, who sacrificed himself for the purpose. I would suppose the story indicates that Aruru began as a goddess of potters, whose primary work is to supply containers of every description. Clay however has been called "the plastic" of the Sumerians, and used to make nearly everything they needed in their culture, not pots alone. The Mesopotamian river valley contained few trees, and no stone or metal. This absence drove the people, tasked with helping the gods, to direct their restless ingenuity, organizational skills, and ambition to make a maximum use of clay, for houses, temples, writing tablets, and storage vessels for honey, wine, beer, oil, butter, water, and dry goods. Credited with the invention of the potter's wheel, the Sumerians created mass production to supply their urban centers, turning their temples into factories for bricks, textiles, and pots. They also undertook a lively trade with other peoples, for wood, gold, copper, semi-precious stones, adding more inventions: hydraulic engineering, the plow, the chariot, metallurgy, and complex mathematics. After the annual river floods, they dredged fertile silt to pour onto their farmland, yet another feat of making abundance from the red-brown and bone-white body of their land herself. Small wonder their creation goddess Aruru would make human beings from clay. At the time I wrote my poem, "To The Mother of All Bowls," I had been invited to participate in an honoring of a friend and longtime colleague, Yoruba Chief Luisah Teish. Already a world-renowned priestess of Oshun, a river deity in Africa and the diaspora, Ye Ye Teish warranted nothing less than a goddess poem. However, though for decades I had saturated my mind with goddess lore, I now had no heart connection to poetry. My full-time job as co-director and faculty of a lively, challenging women's spirituality master's program, and also an arts program, left me no space inside for creative writing of any type, least of all the demanding concentration of poetry. Like the Sumerian cosmic gods, my responsibilities left me needing some help with the honoring gift. The honoring ceremony was on a Saturday afternoon. By Wednesday evening I was frantic, so I prayed for assistance, and at six o'clock in the morning awakened with the entire poem, "To The Mother of All Bowls," in my head. I hope after writing the words down in awe and gratitude, that I also paused to utter the Sumerian prayer sometimes written in clay tablets at the end of a poem, "and praises to Nisaba, goddess of writing."

Marianela Medrano

ATABERYA

In the divine's womb we hug;
a juicy and warm hug.
We sleep the century's long dream
to awake beautiful for the Areito;
so beautiful and forgotten,
enchanting men
with Atabeyra's sacred veil;
with the foamy juice of her saliva
we bring the forest here.

Cave of the Jagua, I came
to wet my lips in black ink,
to then kiss careless lovers
and bring them back to life.
I give them a bone,
to bite in the soft slice of death.

In Atabeyra's warm womb
we drink the elixir of eternity.
The obscure mantle engenders fish,
water. The blue, long current
gives birth to all of us.
There is no Word, only sweetness.
There is no thought,
only the century's feeling.
An exact language;
this pleasure of being born among bones
and the hair of dancing waves,
clear and divine instinct.

Who give birth to the woman I am?
Seashells and sand,
bone and genius in a miracle,
cave and darkness, birth me.
Atabeyra, only Mother,
caressing my dark and tender skin.

ABOUT ATABERYA

I choose Atabeyra or Atabey, the Great Mother in the Taíno cosmogony for this exaltation of the Goddess, to reclaim her name and that of my people. Atabey is worshipped as a goddess of fresh water and fertility. She is also the Earth and water spirit (lakes, streams, the sea, and the marine tides). My work is focused on reclaiming Taíno spirituality which was lost in the patriarchal telling of our history, in the acts of erasure of colonization.

The word Taíno means "good people" in the Arawak language. Taínos were inhabiting the Caribbean Antilles (Cuba, Puerto Rico and the Dominican Republic) at the arrival of European colonization in the XV century.

My interest as a scholar is to examine whether the assumption and knowledge of a Divine Feminine in the Taíno culture can continue to empower Dominican women. I believe that similar culture-specific empowerment can be translated to other women across the globe.

Ann Filemyr

BRIGID

When winter grows weary, Brigid advances
Her green hands rise up out of cold dirt
Her green eyes open, the dawn birds sing
Her green feet mark the meandering of Spring –
Brigid, you are the green flame leaping skyward
the green leaf welling up –

You return flower for flower

Inspiring my Resilience –

Let me follow your Green Way
Walk in the breath-path of your exhalations
Unfurl beneath your pale green cloak

My Green Mother God
as you soften each dry branch
Soften me

for I need you
as I need
to melt
to flame
to flower
to burn
Brighter

Brigid, Sunstar, Daughter-Ancestor
Blood of my Veins, Voice of my Urge
Give me the Courage to Be as I Am

Spinning Wheel
Birth me, Make me new
Again
and Again
as I Turn and Re-Turn –

Light the Kindling
Heaped up Here
in the Cave of my Heart

Brigid Fire
Devour my whittling grief

Burn the refuse
of my resistance
Bathe me in the Deep
Waters of your Well

Teach me to Live
to Love
as Fully and Completely
as that Round Ball of Fire

Gleaming
in your Emerald Breast

ABOUT BRIGID

I choose Brigid, and She chooses me. I celebrate her Holy Day, Imbolc, on February 2 each year. It is the midpoint between Winter Solstice and Spring Equinox in the northern hemisphere, a turning point in the spinning wheel of the annual solar cycle that helps me understand that no matter how hard the darkest, coldest moment, the shift is coming, the light and warmth returning.

Brigid is a Celtic Goddess of poetry, fire, healing, and the fertile return of Spring. She represents the seed sprouting, the first flower, the courage to carry forth, the stamina to sustain. I am descended from Irish-Catholic immigrants, and Brigid is a deity who survived the Roman invader's Christian religion by morphing into Saint Brigid. This meant her eternal flame and Sacred Well became Catholic Holy Places that have been maintained despite the mass conversion of the Celtic people. Brigid's Cross is a pre-Christian symbol signifying the centrality of Here/Now spiraling out into the Life/Death/Rebirth cycle of continuous existence. Reeds or grasses are woven into Four Directions/Four Seasons/Four Spokes/Four Ages. I often make a Brigid's Cross during my Imbolc Ceremony.

Richelle Slota

THE PRAYER OF CYBELE'S
TRANSGENDER PRIESTESSES

In the name of the Mother,
And of the Daughter,
And of the Holy Nymphs.

Hail Cybele,
Protector of Rome
Great Mother of the Gods.

Hail Cybele, full of grace,
(Transgender Goddess,
Ere stripped for parts.)

Surprised the gods are with thee.
Blessed art thou among women,
And blessed is the fruit

Of thy appropriated womb, Mary.
Holy Cybele,
Mother of Gods,

Pray for us sinless,
Now, and at the hour
Of our loving death. Amen.

ABOUT CYBELE

As a transgender woman who grew up praying to the Virgin Mary, I am drawn to Cybele, the Great Mother of the Gods (stripped for parts to make Mary), who was born with male and female genitalia, before being castrated, and who was served by transgender priestesses (i.e., eunuchs).

Cybele originated in Asia Minor. According to myth, Cybele's male and female genitalia scared the gods, so the gods castrated her. In one version of the myth, they discarded her penis which grew into an almond tree. A woman plucked its fruit which made her pregnant with Attis who, in turn, became Cybele's lover. When Attis was unfaithful to Cybele, Attis castrated himself out of anger at himself. Thus, Cybele's eunuch priests also castrated themselves.

Cybele arrived among the Greeks in the 5thCentury, BCE, when a temple to Cybele was built in Athens. The Greeks identified her with Rhea, Mother of the Olympians, and Demeter, the goddess of the harvest.

The cult reached Rome by the end of the 3rd century, BCE, during the Second Punic War. The Roman Senate consulted a book of prophecy which predicted Rome would be saved by a goddess, many interpreted to be Cybele. Indeed, that's what happened: Hannibal suddenly packed up and went back to Carthage. Thus, a temple to Cybele was built on the Palatine Hill.

Cybele was known to the Romans as the Great Mother or Magna Mater. She was very popular among average Romans, especially women. She was mistress of wild nature, symbolized by her constant companion, the lion. She was a healer and a goddess of fertility and a protector in time of war. She was seen as chaste, beautiful, and kind. Followers of her cult would work themselves into frenzies and self-mutilate, symbolic of Attis. Cybele's priests were eunuchs. However, up until the reign of Claudius, Roman law stated that no one could maintain his citizenship if he became a eunuch.(A law we today might identify as anti-transgender. I imagine her temples and her priests as being refuges for transgender women.)

The goddess with the greatest influence on early Christianity, according to Stephen Benko in *The Virgin Goddess, Studies in the Pagan and Christian Roots of Mariology*, 2004, was that of Cybele. Thus, the earth-mother-goddesses were projected onto Mary with little alteration. Benko states, "Christianity did not add a new element to religion when it introduced into its theology such concepts as 'virgin and 'mother'; rather, it sharpened and refined images that already existed in numerous forms in pagan mythology.... there is a direct line, unbroken and clearly discernible, from the goddess cults of the ancients to the reverence paid and eventually the cult accorded to the Virgin Mary."

The idea that Mary is a version of Cybele led me to strip the Hail Mary for parts on Cybele's behalf, because, certainly in this case, turnabout is fair play.

Anna Halberstadt

WHAT THE GODS WERE DOING

When the shtetl Jews were
taken to sunlit woods
in Moletai, Utena or Kaishiadoris
and they were told to dig a pit,
Medeina, the goddess of woods,
looked upon this in disbelief
and horror,
tall Baltic pines swayed in the wind
Saule hid behind the clouds
and covered her beautiful face
with her hands.

But Dalia, the giver of material goods,
stayed and watched the shooting
and a leering man played harmonica
in the background
to silence the screams.
And she watched young trade school students
grab the money,
watches and better clothes
from the naked women and men
lying in the pit,
some still moving and moaning.
One of young Lithuanians
told the Jewish musician
to give him his violin
because he won't need it anyway.

Then Dalia cursed the murderers—
three generations of their
descendants would suffer
from depression, anger and shame,
they will forever deny

complicity with the Nazis,
blame the victims
and lie to their own children
about the provenance
of the better furniture
or the old oak piano in their apartment
or perhaps the Swiss watch
with an inscription from
a grateful patient
taken from the Jewish doctor's wrist.

Bystanders watched silently
when in Vilnius, called Wilno in Polish,
Jews were walked to Ponary
by guards with white armbands
like silent bystanders
who watched us at the Gay Pride parade
in Vilnius in two thousand thirteen.
You could not guess
what they were feeling,
staring at us: tourists,
students and expats,
young and old.

Like they stared at the Jews from the ghetto
on Strashuno street
where my childless aunt Alta
lived after the war,
being taken to their deaths.
In Ponary there is a children's pit
in which two hundred and fifty children
were murdered.
Distraught Laima tried to save
a few pregnant women
but they had no place to run.
When the shooting ended,

a miracle baby, about eighteen months old,
who survived
was playing on the dead bodies of others.
One of the killers
looked at the little boy
and took his rifle off his shoulder
one more time.

Lithuanian Fates—seven sisters, goddesses,
who weave and spin the threads of life,
and make clothes from human lives,
were overwhelmed.
Gadintoja, who tears the thread, and Nukirpeja, who cuts
the cloth of life,
threw their scissors to the ground and cried.
Perkunas, God of Thunder,
sat on top of his tall mountain
and watched what his people had done
in silence
with the magic bow, which fires bolts of lightning,
frozen in his hand.

ABOUT DALIA

Dalia is the goddess of fate in Lithuanian mythology, sometimes depicted as a woman, sometimes as a trinity—three women, weaving and cutting threads of life. It may be confusing, since there are seven goddesses of fate, similar to Moiras and Parkas in other writings on Lithuanian mythology. She sometimes appears as a lamb, dog, swan or duck, as well. Dalia, which means fate in Lithuanian, is also the giver and taker of material goods. She is concerned with material wealth the person would earn during his/her lifetime. It is known, that perpetrators of the Holocaust in Lithuania, where there were 150,000 Jewish homes before the war, allowed the volunteers, many of them young students of trade schools, take belongings of the Jews they were killing. It is well documented how Lithuanians, most of them peasants, benefited from taking homes, furniture, musical instruments, clothes etc., of the victims. So in my poem Dalia, who is watching the events is the essential goddess, who normally is the enforcer of the will of Dievas or Perkunas, who is similar to Zeus.

Annie Finch

FOR *FRIJA,
WHEREVER I MAY FIND YOU

*Frija, I find you   falling around me
I grasp the gold   of your guiding thread
Shapeshifting weaver   spinning with stars

*Frija, I learn you   leading within me
Strong in my vulva   your visions build
Life-changing weaver   lifting the stars

*Frija, I take you   turning beside me
Your joyful halls   harvest me home
Ritual weaver   rocking the stars

ABOUT *FRIJA

A few years before my mother died, we did a DNA test and found she was almost completely Nordic. I was shocked; we had always thought she was Scottish. I started exploring Norse Shamanism, and the practices moved me to the core. To choose a Norse Goddess to encounter in my poem for *An Exaltation of Goddesses* felt natural. But I was overwhelmed. Patriarchy was deep-rooted among the Norse; their Goddesses feel like some of the most distorted, damaged, and disappeared of all. There was so much healing and recovery to be done. I tried to use existing poems about Sumerian or Celtic Goddesses instead. Both were chosen by other contributors, and so I accepted my path.

But which Goddess? The two central Norse Goddesses, Freya and Frigg, are almost absurdly similar. Their magical necklaces have the same name, and so do their husbands; each of them wears a falcon-feather shapeshifting cloak and has power over weaving, spinning, prophecy, childbirth, and sexuality. In most of Northern Europe, it turns out, they are treated as the same Goddess.

But the Norse pantheon treats them as two. And a main difference between them is that Frigg is a serene Goddess of marriage and motherhood, while Freya is a wild Goddess of promiscuous sex. Patriarchal religion has a pattern of dividing Goddesses into dutiful wives and dangerous whores, and I had no patience for these stereotypes. No wonder that when I began to write poems to Freya or Frigg, they went nowhere.

Then I learned about *Frija, whom scholars think may have been the common ancestor of Freya and Frigg. *Frija wears an asterisk before her name because she's hypothetical. I love this. My Muse is turned on by mystery and secrets and loves to explore new places. I dove into the poem enthusiastically and felt *Frija reaching out to me in return, bringing together the qualities of Freya and Frigg. As I healed my own divide between madonna and whore, both of us seemed to be homing into each other, shrugging aside the fogs of patriarchal lies and silence.

*Frija spins the thread of the universe on her distaff made of the stars of Orion's belt. Like many sun goddesses, she spins gold thread. She also spins the clouds. She makes sacred the power of erotic love, birth control, midwifery, childbirth, and death; the dead feast with her on an island in the sea. She understands and rules magic, ritual, and destiny, though she usually keeps her knowledge quiet. She is also the Goddess of legal contracts and agreements. The author Hearth Moon Rising points out that Frigg may have invented writing and the system of Norse runes; she is closely associated with the birch tree, whose bark was used for writing in northern Europe.

My poem's form would be familiar to *Frija. It is written in the accentual alliterative verse traditional to Nordic poetry. Each line has four strongly accented syllables and a pause in the middle, with at least one initial consonant repeating across the half-lines.

Purvi Shah

HELD BY FIVE NERVES, YOUR TONGUE VERGES ON FIRE

Your tongue speaks better as pencil.

The graphite roots, the molten cloud.
The syllables escaping —   char of vibrations.

Kali wanted the world charcoal
so even fire would know its burn.

In smoke, the roots of speech simmer
as red vine. There's even a six-

fingered hand pushing thought forward. (That extra   finger which got chopped
off to make girl.) In our roots, a calendula

growing, unseen thorns twisted like blood
            inside out.

Kali prefers an endpoint, that full stop you dotted
the page with, that attempt to make the thought close —

        A now, no

         longer.

You fear absorption — black palate stretching.
You write: I crossed the bridge. I bridged.

Shave pencil & volcano oozes. Reach into middle earth,
  where nerves end in a calendula growing.

    In the dark there is no destiny — only movement

ABOUT KALI

 Kali moves through this poem as goddess of destruction, as mother of aliveness, as women's warrior, as force generating word & page, as vibration, as energy, as everything.

Arundhati Subramaniam

GODDESS
(AFTER LINGA BHAIRAVI)

In her burning rainforest
silence is so alive
you can hear
listening.

GODDESS
(AFTER LINGA BHAIRAVI)

She sucks you
into the raging blue wilderness
of her womb
where you wear her
like cocoon,
you wear her
like cosmos,
through which you reel,
exuberantly
Unborn.

GODDESS
(AFTER NEELI MARIAMMAN)

*'It's enough / to sit alone / and gaze at you / three-eyed God-
dess. / Who needs to go meditate?' – Abhirami Bhattar (translated
from the Tamil)*

Those who go to the great temples
of Perur and Avinashi
know nothing of her.
She's isn't interested

in being the flavour
of a few thousand years.

She's been around
since the planet was a seizure

of waterness
and protoplasm.

In the great garrulity of gods
she is silent.

She'll never be the life
of the party

but she's not concerned with the party.

She is life --
twisty blue nerve fire --

life local,
life perennial,

     the goddess Neeli Mariamman.

On Tuesday afternoons
in the month of May

she erupts
into an epilepsy of form,

ballooning a small nut-brown priest
into prescience,

and as he foams and curdles,
his eyes sightless,

she prescribes remedies
to a peasant plagued
by blisters in his gum,

advises the crone to be patient
with her daughter–in-law

for women must be wooed
and fear must not spawn a new generation.

Then she turns towards you
and her eyes are craters,

her light molten jaggery
and burnt almond,

her tongue is toxic shock,
her gaze tundra.

She is the shockingly naked wire
at the centre of the world

where your future is a long burnt-out
morning star.

The universe is her hamlet,
she says,

a flystain
in her monarchy.

Her laughter is her empire.

ABOUT LINGA BHAIRAVI AND
NEELI MARIAMMAN

When I first entered the Linga Bhairavi shrine, I expected coconuts, watering eyes and some visual beauty. But little else. And yet, something stirred at that first meeting. She became my personal goddess – my *ishta devi*, as it were – very soon after that.

Fierce, intense, alive, and protective, Linga Bhairavi transports me to some primal place of origin—a womb, a sanctuary, comforting, energizing, nurturing, vitalizing, all at once. For those who don't lean towards anthropomorphic notions of the divine, she is a mercury linga with three-and-a-half chakras, a device for physical, psychological and spiritual well being. But for the devotional, the heart-centred, she is nothing less than the primal mother.

For me, she is a reminder that materiality and *moksha* aren't at odds. She reminds me that the journey from samsara to nirvana can be harmonious, organic, non-disruptive. That the life journey is intended to be luminous, abundant, auspicious. That the human being is not intended to be a walking civil war, but an integrated, cohesive entity—a breathing shrine.

In my recent book *Women Who Wear Only Themselves*, I wrote of her: 'She has been the lubricant, the ally at my elbow, the whisper in my ear, the voice of my heart that told me that the inner world and the outer,… aren't at war. I know Devi as a deity who lives in a temple. I also know her as inner experience… As deity, she is explosively engaged. She is unafraid to… engage herself in the minutiae of your life. She loves the particular. She loves the singular. She is universality itself. And yet, she surges between the abstract and concrete with an impunity, with a gorgeous elegance – the kind that, I suppose, only a goddess would be capable of.'

The shrine of Neeli Mariamman, on the other hand, is a little-known site I stumbled upon some years ago. As I sat there, I began to experience her as an unmistakable presence: fluid, throbbing, quietly intoxicating. Her handkerchief-sized temple is manned by a tribal priest. When he is 'possessed' by his goddess, however, this small, soft-spoken little man is transformed into a vast presence, red-eyed and foaming, clairvoyant and compassionate.

I have long marveled at how many local goddesses exist in south India, unsung and undocumented. And it began to feel necessary to speak of Neeli Mariamman in verse, to usher this little-known morsel of divinity into the world of Indian Anglophone poetry. And so, I did.

She is a part of my new poetry collection, *Love Without a Story*. 'Those who go to the great temples/ of Perur and Avinashi/ know nothing of her…,' I wrote in my invocation to her. 'She isn't interested/ in being the flavor/ of a few thousand years …In the great garrulity of gods/ she is silent./ She will never be the life of the party/ But she's not concerned with the party./ She is life —/ twisty blue nervefire,/ life local,/ life perennial,/ the goddess Neeli Mariamman.'

I hope to sing of the many goddesses of south India again.

Yona Harvey

NANA BURUKU

Because you are older than God, some
say you cannot be called upon. Because you are
older than God, we call on you.

Androgynous Mother of Mawu & Lisa,
Moon & Sun, they say your Twins
do your bidding. But through the ice
of our lapsed memories, you saw us—
our glass cages, our earthly rages,
our earthbound hair.

We were once stone-cold women
claiming flawlessness. Though none of us
believed. Our embraces were all elbows
& lower arms—no muscle, no flesh in them.
We were shy about creation. No, we were
confused about it.

You live in the blood & hum
of elder women, the ones who keep metal
from offerings where we stand naked
without our usual, beautiful weapons.

ABOUT NANA BURUKU

During the difficult months of COVID-19 I began thinking about who and what I choose rather than who or what I resist. Because of schedule changes and spending more time indoors, I had more time for reading. The words of Audre Lorde and Lucille Clifton mingled in my thoughts. Lorde wrote of Dahomey (Benin) and women's divine powers. And Rachel Harding noted in her essay "Authority, History, and Everyday Mysticism in the Poetry of Lucille Clifton: A Womanist View" how she observed Nana Buruku's presence in Clifton's poems. Finding information about Nana Buruku has been difficult. But I feel blessed in learning this "energy of creation" as Harding calls her, lives "in the myths of Afro-Brazilian Candomblé" and across the African Diaspora in Nigeria, Benin, and the Caribbean. She is a protector of women who does not tolerate "being crossed." She embodies the moon and sun (her twin children Mawu and Lisa), and is the mother of Oshun. She is also considered the Orisha of epidemics and disease, which feels timely. I'm intrigued by the fact that she is often portrayed as an elderly woman or grandmother, as The Creator. Women are creators. And it is with gratitude to Lorde, Clifton, and Harding I choose to pay homage.

Raina Leon

FROM THE ADYTON

nyx who stood at creation's dark dawn, blinking her
eyes into a wind whisper, takes human form, fills the fleshy
folds of it with languor. she widens the hips with death,
shimmies her swagger so those who see long for an end
that starts in her. from her ear lobes, she hangs pearls to
counter the tacky tar allure of her eyes. her scent blooms
in summer-sweated jasmine. she lives beyond ocean or
light, beyond time's witness of dusty mounding into the
body that entangles with body and dissembles some day
after many days into dust. she sparked creation in dream
and holds it thrumming to bleat. she perches maternal, at
the edge of metaphoric devouring. her skin prickles with
an ever-primed mother fury: don't. touch. my. baby. not
his hair. not her body. not their anything. not them. what is
not hers, that she has borne and not born? nothing can be
touched and truly known. she most definitively is black, god
and feared by gods, loved for her whole night in its schism
memories.

ABOUT NYX

The name, Nyx, fascinated me when I first heard it used for a character on the sci-fi show, Dark Matter. Being the inquisitive person I am, I went through warp holes (rather than rabbit holes) to discover more about the name, Nyx. I did not know until that search that she was a goddess, primordial and elemental, there at at the dawn of creation and before, feared by all gods who came after for her power, her maternal fierceness, the threat and promise of the dark. There is a lesson with Nyx and, in my mind, her connection with black mothering, actually so many lessons, that I stand in frequent regard of her as icon.

Monica Mody

SARASVATI

Not the slick but the tumbling
                    goddess
                             river

tresses matted
mud and water

            Coltish, sometimes—
legs, arms
            scratched from running through rushes

Dight in jute, droplets
around neck
                    syllables, words,
                     all names, all creation

River whose waters billow with hymns

Inspirer of thought

Giver of eloquence
            Life's full-bodied vital veena

Hamsini

Sarasvati
            of irrepressible luminosity

            You changed
for every age—
Who will you become for ours?

We need your wisdom foremost

Your adamantine
gaze that disarms lies

Sun glitter
sparkling under volar
forearm skin

Limned, like every divinity,
by landscape

(gravel, mollusk)

You emerge from gates of heaven
bearing good gifts in life waters

Radiant and swift

Mighty with waves

Supple
with discrimination

In you is all flow, all
creation

Time
slips like silk
cyclical, continuous

Dawn-goddess of understanding

Liberate consciousness
from disconnected thinking

Grant us amrita—
capacity to see

entangled connections of life

Vageeswari

Why aren't we talking, still, about women
that beaded breathfuls
            —inspiration
on your banks?

Sarasvati, have you
turned to sludge

impetuousness buried
under strata
            (patriarchy)

In this age of human exceptionalism—
surrendered morals—
is it perilous
            invoking you?

The people of India
scramble for footholds
            in our own mythic pasts

Ancestral stores
            stories
appropriated by miscreants
            hearts hardened
                        with hate

Your sacred name weaponized
to erase people and histories

You keep your secret
coiled underground
                naga-like—

on a standby, perhaps,
or dreaming—

below earth that soaked
libations

Where fierce waters
carried hymns to ocean once

you bleed underground—
premonition of what has come to be

Grief scrapes my hands
                into pincers
rooting for river fragments—

                dried tears—gnarled roots—

Tongue, its own agent,
ululates

                setting aside its thieves
                I fall/flow

When your children turn coin-faced
we keep losing
                braid of twine—

skies thin—

still, like serum

you test our strength

hum in ear

slip like silk in measure of time

Goddess of craft and grace

pluck a new story
on our strings

Discernment,
                knowing
flowing to right
speech, mysteries
of sound and intent—
            action

Teach us to generate
frameworks we wish to see

Bestow on us nectar of memory,
understanding, creative power

that this subterranean
reemerges
            river of wisdom

ABOUT SARASVATI

What does it mean to write a poem about Sarasvati now of all times? What is she asking of us? What can we ask of her?

In South Asia, unlike in the West, the goddess did not disappear—she continues to be venerated in the living tradition, which has developed varied theologies in relation to her. The goddess has many forms, many names through the length and the breadth of the land. As a signifier, she has often been cherry-picked by caste-based patriarchy and reactionary Hindu nationalism for ends that skitter far away from spiritual meaning. This makes the discursive field around goddess-centered spirituality contentious for artists and scholars located within contemporary contexts of social change in South Asia.

Sarasvati, considered to be the presiding deity of learning and the arts, is an important goddess in the Hindu pantheon—finding a significant place even in Buddhist and Jain pantheons. While writing this poem, even as I wanted to invoke the qualities of wisdom Sarasvati embodies, I wanted to bring in my ambivalence about the ideals of femininity—specifically for women of words, a way of being cultured—portrayed in her iconography and mythology, reinforcing a Brahmanical epistemology of perfection and purity.

To trouble these representations, I turned to the imagery of her as a river. In my poem, Sarasvati is still wild. In the Rig Veda, Sarasvati is spoken of as a 'mighty' and 'uncontrollable' river; later texts describe her as a 'disappearing' river who becomes 'invisible'. This is not a poem in which I chart the journey of the river's disappearance, or that of the river goddess becoming the goddess of knowledge, even as—following the work of scholars including Catherine Ludvik—I see the mysteries of the later transformation encoded within associations, noted in the Rig Veda, of the river goddess with *dhi* (inspired thought) and with *vac* (speech).

I also wanted the poem to acknowledge that, for Hindutva, finding the lost river Sarasvati has become a *svarna mriga* (golden deer)—a lure through which they seek to assert the civilizational superiority of 'Aryavarta'—the land of the Aryans. I wanted to explore if there is a different possibility that an invocation of Sarasvati could raise.

In terms of form, I was thinking of Enheduanna's use of the first person in the hymn, "Exaltation of Inanna"— how she interweaves a cultural, political, and personal narrative with the praise of Inanna. I was attentive to the ecology of sound within the poem, especially since Sarasvati embodies the power of sound.

Bibliography

Abraham, Shirley, and Amit Madheshiya. "A Mythical River Flows Through Indian Politics." *The New York Times*, 10 July 2018.

Danino, Michel. *The Lost River: On the Trail of the Sarasvati.* Penguin, 2010.

Ghosh, Niranjan. *Srí Sarasvatí in Indian Art and Literature*. Sri Satguru Publications, 1984.

Kinsley, David R. *Hindu Goddesses: Visions of the Divine Feminine in the Hindu Religious Tradition.* Berkeley: University of California Press, 1986.

Ludvik, Catherine. *Sarasvatí: Riverine Goddess of Knowledge*. Brill, 2007.

Shaw, Miranda E. *Buddhist Goddesses of India*. Princeton, N.J: Princeton University Press, 2006.

Mary Mackey

SONG FOR RAISING A GODDESS STONE

AN INVOCATION TO XORI,
OWL GODDESS OF BRITTANY

Lift Her up!
Lift the Great Owl
who blesses us all.
Lift Her up
so the dead can rest
under Her wings.
Lift Her up!
Worship Her with your strength.

ABOUT XORI

Xori, The Owl Goddess of Brittany is an aspect of the Bird Goddess of Old Europe. The poem; "Song for Raising a Goddess Stone" from my novel *The Year The Horses Came*, is about the Goddess Worshiping People of Old Europe.

Jurgita Jasponyté

THE ENCHANTMENTS OF EARTH.
NEW MOON

> Sidabro lakiùté
> Sidabro.
> Sutartinéùfrom Paringys

1

 As if one is invited,
one is called
as if the vectors of windrows
point north
and the thoughts of the earth awaken
so that you know
what actions to take.

A thread freezes and breaks in the cold –
The stalk of a nascent moon.

2

I am tired
of holding my tongue,
everything must be said,
quickly,
while the seed is sown –

magic words
enchant the earth
and you can't
prevent life
as your palms enclose roots
lifting everything
up

until I am cleansed by my own abnegation
until fear-filled eyes put me to the test.

3

Protect us from the rain
that promises more
than we need,
give us enough mouths
if you set the harvest upon us
through the fields

I know you are my mother,
that my legs are stuck in you
for ages,
and to break away
promises only
another turning towards you

I know that we love you
not just for
your ear for our prayers,
your gift of the harvest,
but how you don't hesitate to feed
the mouth that disrespects you,
that fails to understand
the what and from where
of life –

your unconditionality
is the most perfect form of truth.

Let there be heaven for us
through rain.

4

In the cold, thread freezes and breaks –
the cord connecting the earth
with the pink moon of morning –
a shield
protecting us –

born naked
every evening.

ABOUT ŽEMYNA

Žemyna (also Žemynélé or Žemelé) (from Lithuanian:
žemé– earth) is the goddess of the earth in Lithuanian religion or Baltic people. She is usually regarded as mother
goddess and one of the chief Lithuanian gods similar to
Latvian Zemes mãte. Žemyna personifies the fertile earth
and nourishes all life on earth, human, plant, and animal.
All that is born of earth will return to earth, thus her cult
is also related to death. As the cult diminished after bap-
tism of Lithuania, Žemyna's image and functions became
influenced by the cult of Virgin Mary. Prätorius described a
ritual, called *žemyneliauti*, performed at major celebrations
(e.g. weddings) or agricultural works (e.g. harvest). The
head of the household would drink a cup of beer, but first,
he would spill some of the drink on the ground and say a
short prayer. People would also kiss the earth saying a short
prayer thanking Žemyna for all her gifts and acknowledging
that one day they will return to her.

In addition, historical sources on Baltic mythology describe the dual role of goddess Zemyna: while she was con-
nected to the fertility of the land, she was also associated
with receiving the dead and acting as their ruler and guard-
ian. Pieces of Lithuanian folklore also make references to
Earth as mother of humans and their final abode after death.

ABOUT THE CONTRIBUTORS

Ann Filemyr, PhD, is President of Southwestern College and Director of the Ecotherapy Certificate. Her books of poetry include *The Healer's Diary* and *The Vowels.*

Annie Finch is an award-winning poet and an editor, critic, playwright, and performer. Her books include *Among the Goddesses* and *Spells: New and Selected Poems.*

Judy Grahn is a poet, author, and cultural theorist whose books deepen goddess studies, take racism personally, and engage psychically with creatures.

Anna Halberstadt is a poet who writes in English and Russian and translates from English, Russian and Lithuanian. She has published six books of poetry.

Yona Harvey is the author of two poetry collections, *Hemming the Water* and *You Don't Have to Go to Mars for Love.*

Jurgita Jasponytė is a Lithuanian poet, author of *Šaltupė* and *The Sharp Gates of Dawn.*

She was awarded the Vilnius Mayor Prize in 2019.

Raina J. León, PhD, is Afro-Boricua, from Philadelphia, the author of three collections of poetry, *Canticle of Idols, Boogeyman Dawn,* and *sombra: dis(locate)*, and a founding editor of *The Acentos Review*

Mary Mackey, PhD, is New York Times best-selling author of eight collections of poetry and fourteen novels including *The Year The Horses Came.* (Harper Collins, 1993)

Marianela Medrano is a Dominican poet and writer living in Connecticut since 1990. She writes in Spanish and English. Her poetry has been translated into Italian and French.

Monica Mody, PhD, is a border-crossing poet and transdisciplinary feminist scholar practicing earth-based decolonial spirituality. She is the author of *Bright Parallel*, *Ordinary Anna*ls, and *Kala Pani*.

Purvi Shah's favorite art practices are sparkly eyeshadow, raucous laughter, and seeking justice. Her new book, *Miracle Marks*, explores women, the sacred, and gender & racial equity.

Richelle Lee Slota writes poetry, novels, non-fiction and plays. She lives in San Francisco and performs a one-transwoman show called *Kind of a Drag*.

Arundhathi Subramaniam is a leading Indian poet and author of twelve books of poetry and prose, most recently *Love Without a Story* (*Bloodaxe Books*, 2020).

ACKNOWLEDGMENTS

Since 2010 when Patricia Monaghan invited my Goddess mask and me to perform at the Association for the Study of Women and Mythology, the knowledge and wisdom I found in this unique community have joyfully recalibrated my life. Special thanks to Sid Reger for your devoted and hardworking leadership of ASWM over many years, for first inciting this project, and for holding space as it grew.

Thanks to Deeksha Vats, who began as my literary assistant and quickly became a magical ally in all things Poetry Witch. Many are grateful for the multivalent talents you share with Poetry Witch Community, Poetry Witch Ritual Theater, and Poetry Witch Press.

Thanks to the artist and poet Diane Lee Moomey for agreeing to help design the book. Your beautiful energy permeates every word.

Thanks to Alicja Barcikowska for generously donating your inspiring and beautiful artwork for the cover of this book and the movie title.

And finally, thanks to all the contributing poets, you who gave so generously of your time and talent to write and perform these precious poems.

Grateful acknowledgment to the following publications in which these poems first appeared:

"To the Mother of All Bowls" by Judy Grahn from *Love Belongs to Those Who do the Feeling* (Red Hen Press, 2008)

"The Enchantments of Earth. New Moon" by Jurgita Jasponytė from *Vartai Austrieji* (Lithuanian Writers' Union Publishing House, 2019)

"Song for Raising a Goddess Stone: Invocation to Xori, Owl Goddess of Brittany" by Mary Mackey from *The Year The Horses Came*, Book I of the *Earthsong Trilogy* (Harper Collins, 1993)

"Ataberya" by Marianela Medrano from *Diosas de la Yuca* (Eciciones Torremozas, Madrid, 2011)

"Held by five nerves, your tongue verges on fire" by Purvi Shah from *Nimrod*.

"Goddesses (after Linga Bhairavi and Neeli Mariam man)" by Arundhati Subramaniam from *Love Without a Story* (Bloodaxe Books, 2019).

ABOUT POETRY WITCH PRESS

The mission of Poetry Witch Press is to serve the needs of Poetry Witch Community; to support the resurgence of the Divine Feminine; and to celebrate and share the crafts of meter, form, and rhythm. For more information please visit poetrywitchpress.com.

ABOUT THE BOOK DESIGN

What a treat it has been to work on the creation of *Exaltation of Goddesses!* Producing a physical book requires making dozens of decisions, both large and small, and at each point-of-choice Annie and I were quickly able to find a path that felt right to both of us. I am honored to be part of this project, and look forward to helping to create more book projects for Poetry Witch Press.

The font we chose is Perpetua, 11 point for the poems and prose, and 12 point for the titles.

Diane Lee Moomey
www.dianeleemoomeyart.com